New Persuasive Art

An

Art style that I've Invented

By

Dejuan Hunt II

Introduction

I've invented a new art style called New Persuasive Art. Captivating your imagery and then cultivating it with another medium. In this new art style it could be multiple papers on canvas depicting a story, and at the same time the artist could chose multiple media over those images, or that image. Persuading the viewers mind to think outside the box the same time. New Persuasive Art.

I've invented a new art style called New Persuasive Art. Captivating your imagery and then culptivating it with other mediums. In this new art style it could be multiple papers on canvas depicting a story, and at the same time the artist. Could chose multiple media over those images, or that image. Persuading the viewers mind to think outside the box the same time. New Persuasive Art

7/24/2015

Chapter 2

As I continue with my technique I also come to realize that the medium doesn't even matter. Rather it be sculpture of any material, or photography, as long as the rules apply the same as what I told you before in the introduction than it is clearly New Persuasive Art. On this chapter I will also show you a few samples of my artwork itself. So you can kind of have an ideal thought to what New Persuasive art is. But keep in mind that these are just a few of my artwork pertaining New Persuasive Art, and that this is not just the medium or material only pertaining to New Persuasive Art. Because there is no limit when it comes to New Persuasive Art, and by saying that. This also means that even a video concerning New Persuasive Art can even be possible.

Images Pertaining New Persuasive Art

From the Artist Dejuan Hunt II

The inventor of the art style

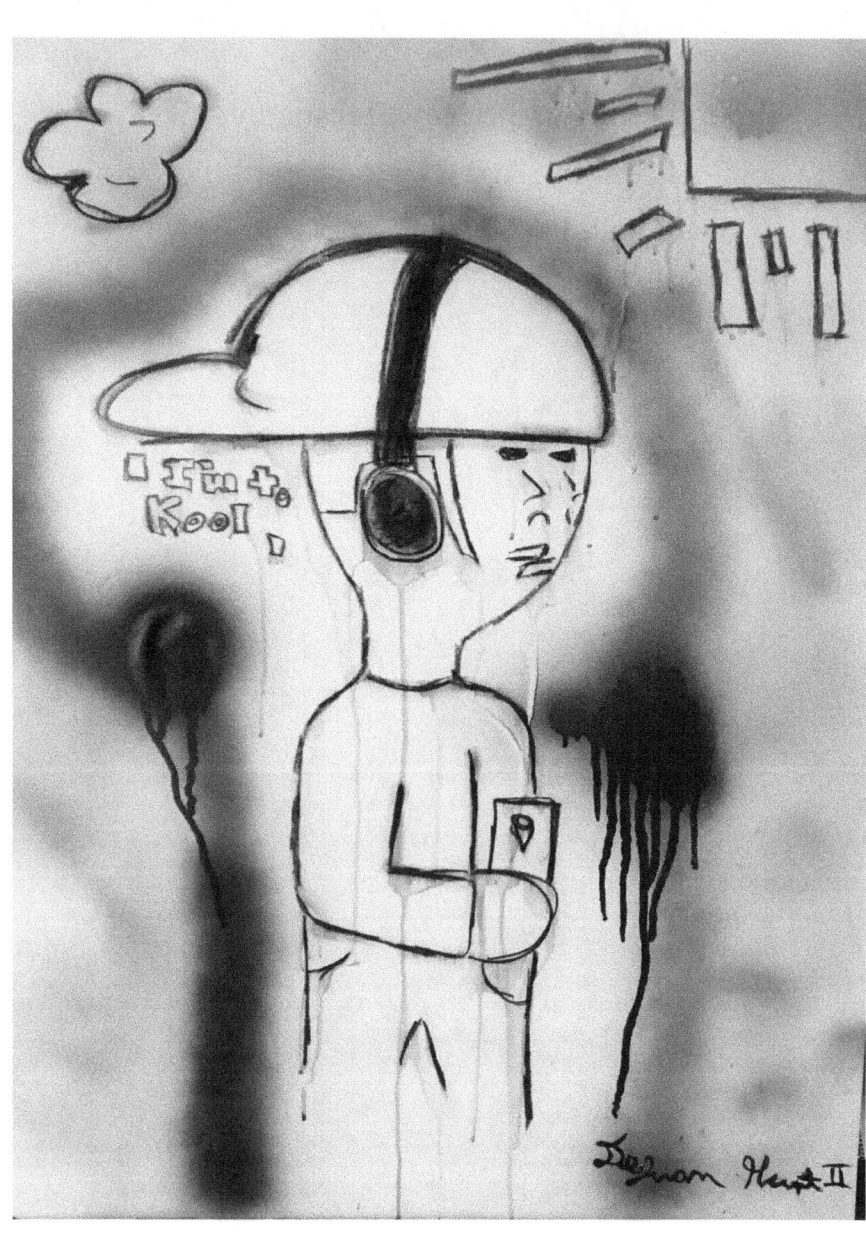

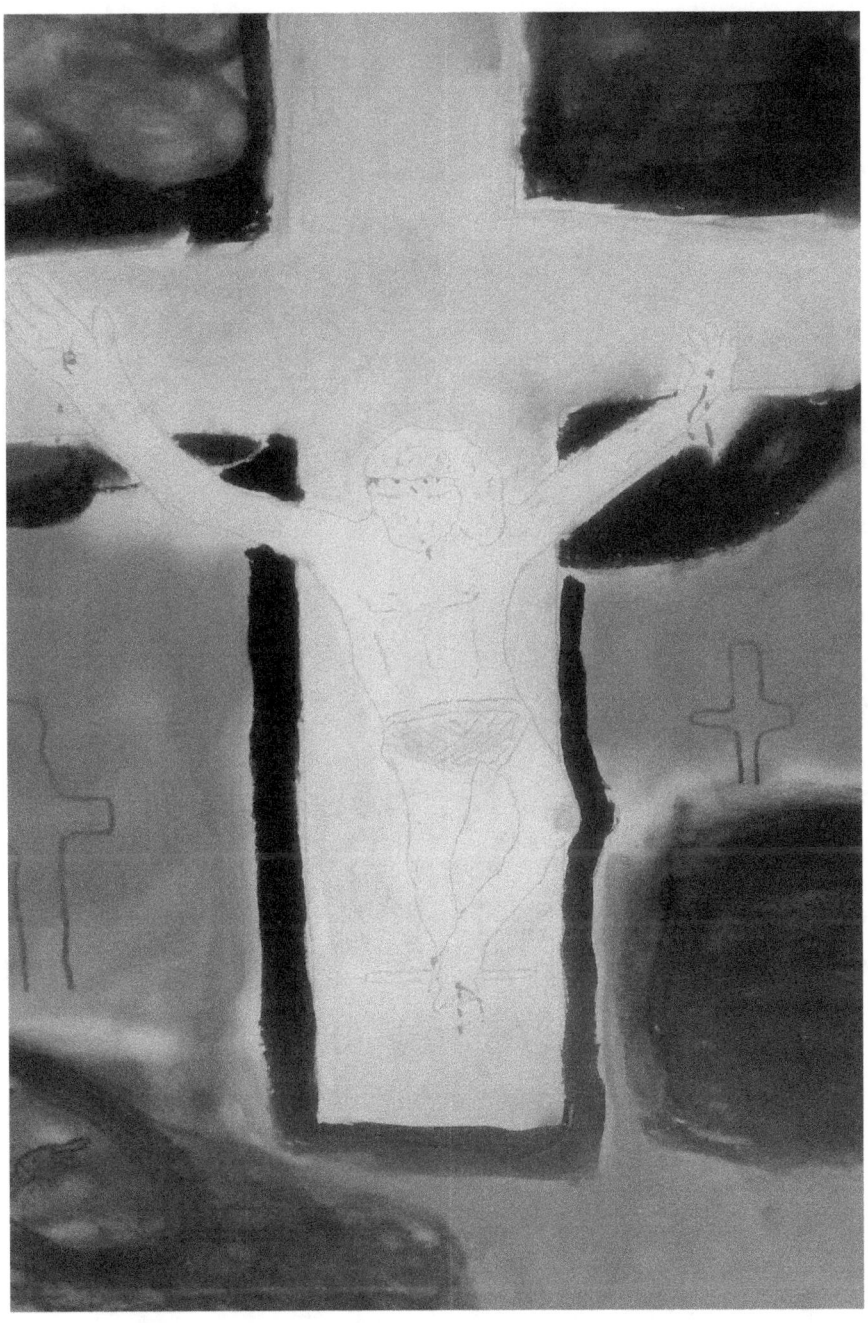

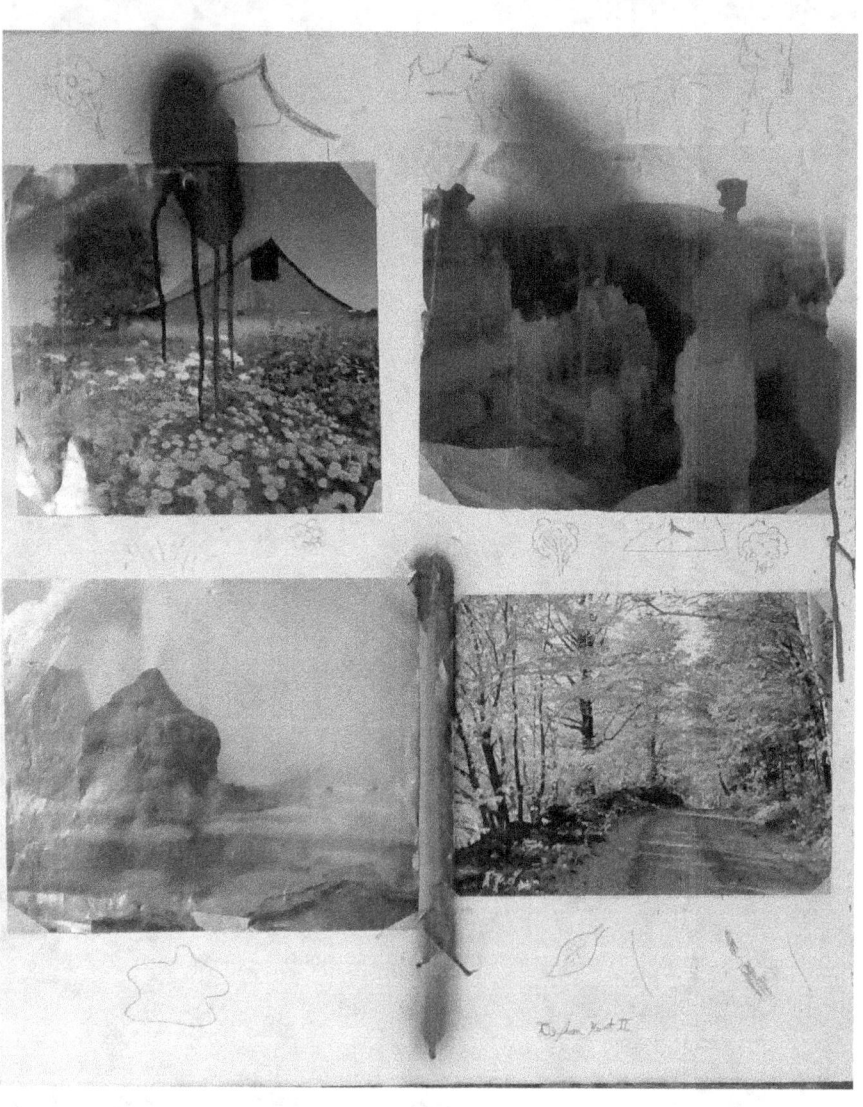

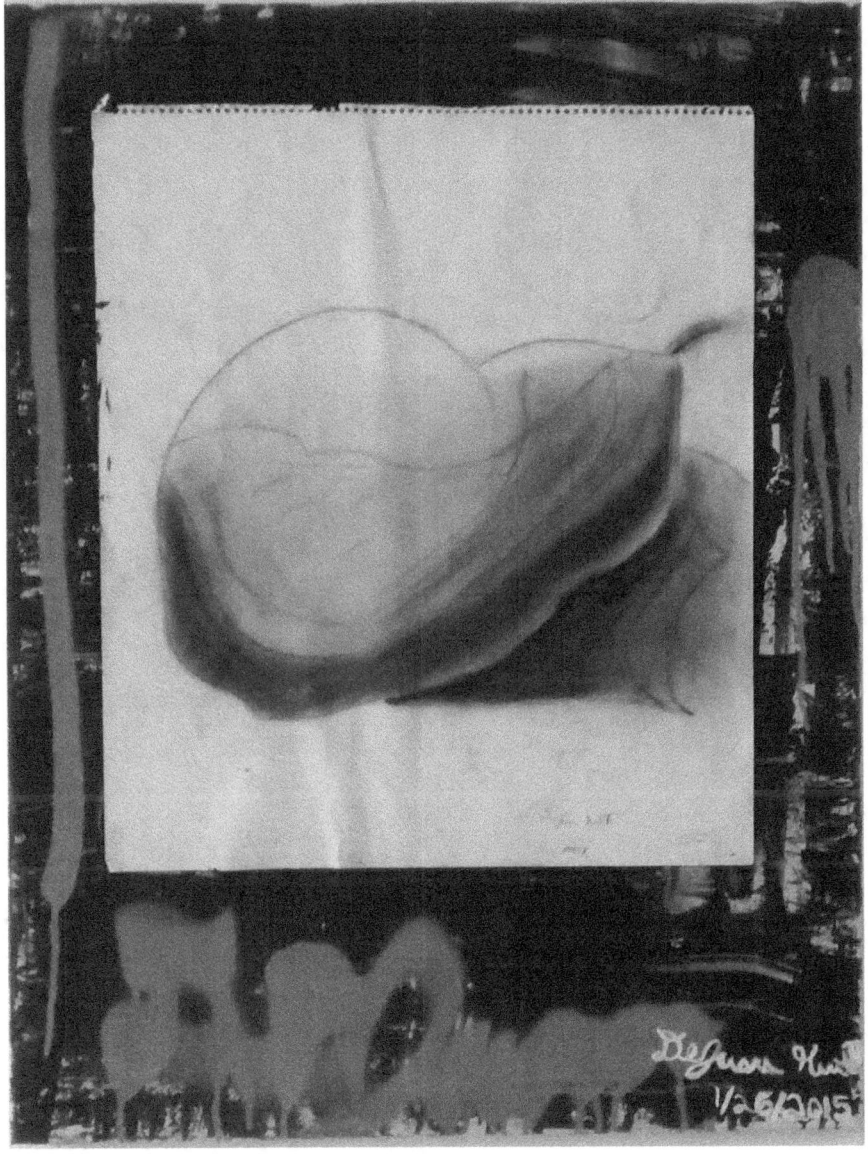

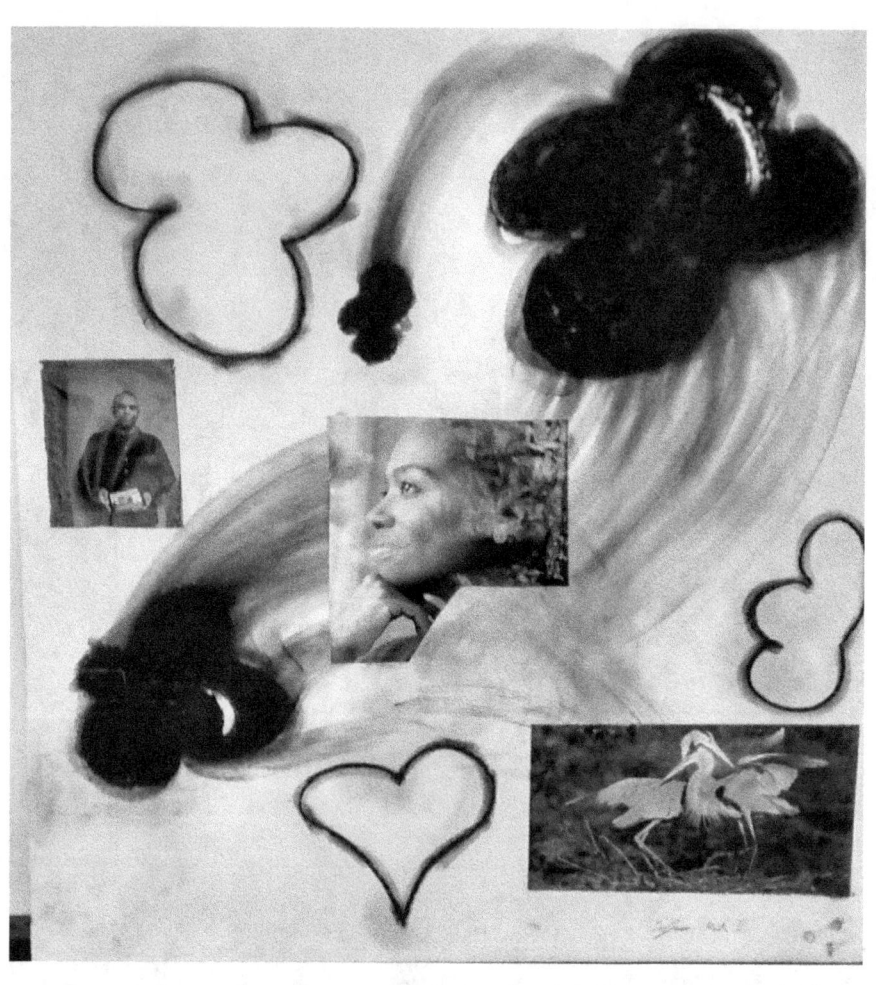

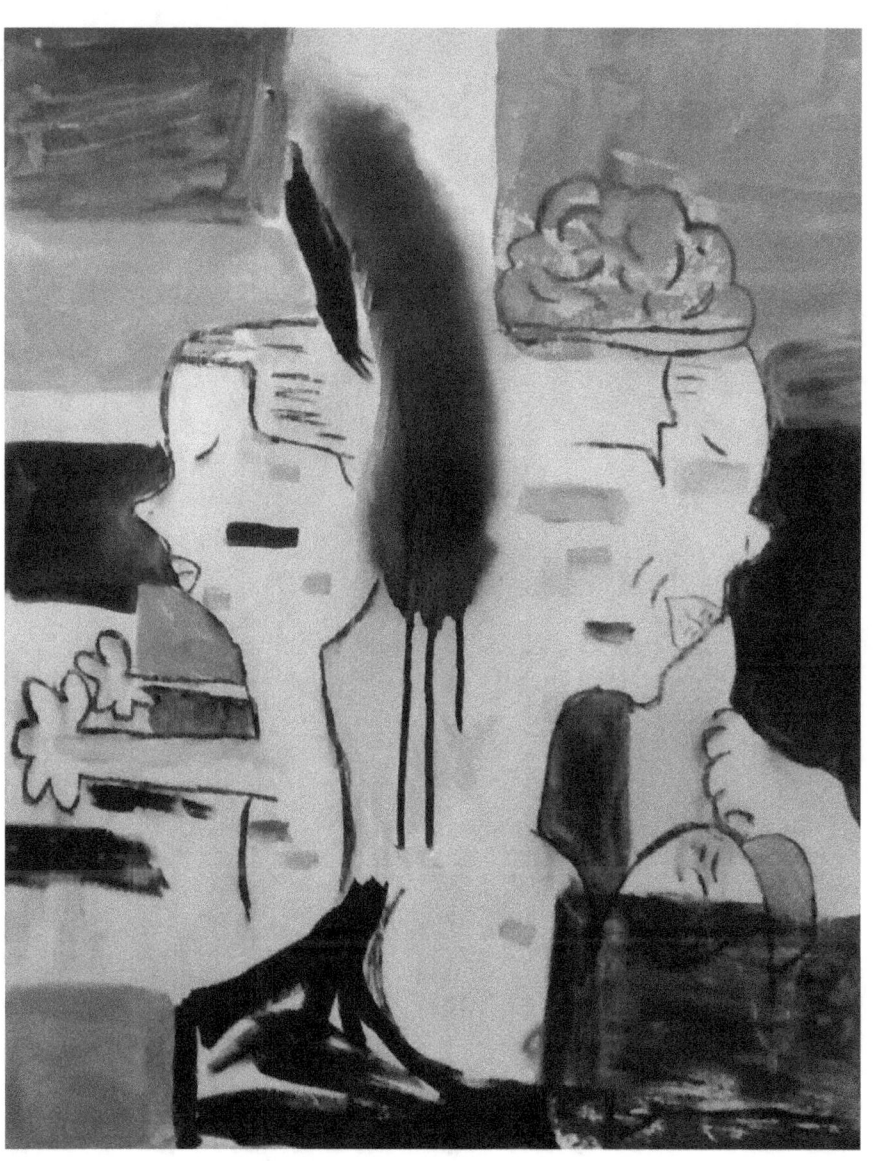

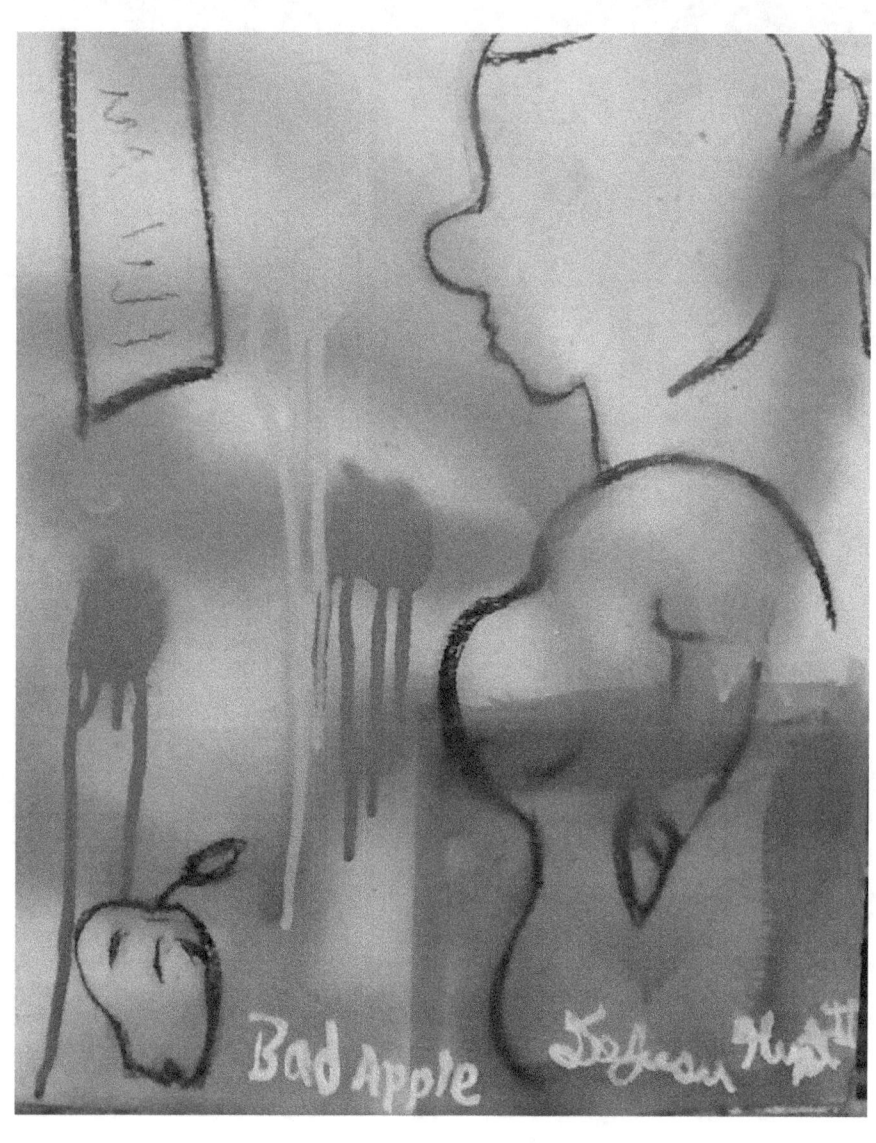

Again these photos are a few examples of the technique called New Persuasive Art. And there is no limit to just how far New Persuasive Art technique can go.

Chapter 3

Using multiple mediums in the art studio, it came a time when I felt that I should make new art style. In some sort of way a, beginning my own trend. I remember when I was a kid going to an art museum and things just appeared to certain people so simple. But now in the times that we are living in right now, some people say somethings aren't so simple. But that might just be there perspective. I'm going to tell you that with New Persuasive Art, it is never simple, but instead the complete opposite.

Notes

_____

_____

_____

_____

_____

_____

_____

_____

Artist Dejuan Hunt II

Message from this Book

I hope you've have gotten a pretty good sense to what New Persuasive Art really is, and do not get it confused with Mixed Media. Because the two styles are completely different. Keep that in mind.

www.ingramcontent.com/pod-product-compliance
Lightning Source LLC
Chambersburg PA
CBHW070759180526
45168CB00004B/1674